# Gentle Gorillas and Other Apes

## By Allan Fowler

**Consultants:**
Robert L. Hillerich, Professor Emeritus,
Bowling Green State University, Bowling Green, Ohio
Consultant, Pinellas County Schools, Florida

Lynne Kepler, Educational Consultant

Fay Robinson, Child Development Specialist

Ⓟ CHILDRENS PRESS®

CHICAGO

Design by Beth Herman Design Associates

**Library of Congress Cataloging-in-Publication Data**

Fowler, Allan.
    Gentle gorillas and other apes / by Allan Fowler.
    p. cm. – (Rookie read-about science)
    ISBN 0-516-06022-8
    1. Apes–Juvenile literature. [1. Apes.] I. Title.
    II. Series: Fowler, Allan. Rookie read-about science.
    QL737.P96F68    1994
    599.88–dc20                                        93-38590
                                                           CIP
                                                            AC

This gorilla is beating on his chest and making a loud, hooting noise.

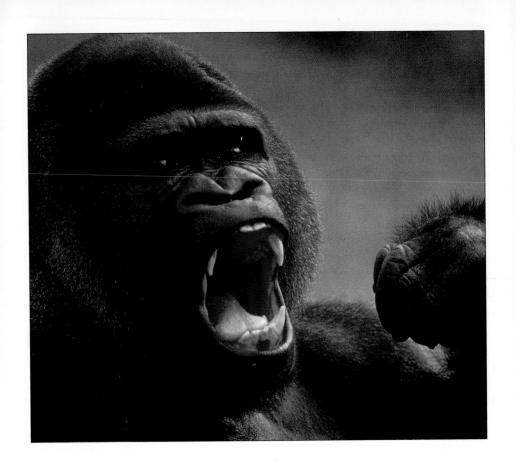

Is he about to attack?
No, he is simply scaring
intruders away.

Gorillas are very strong,
but they are also gentle.

Gorillas are apes – the largest apes of all.

Apes belong to a family of animals called primates.

Monkeys are also primates.

So are human beings.

All primates have fingers,
and many have thumbs.
They can hold onto things.

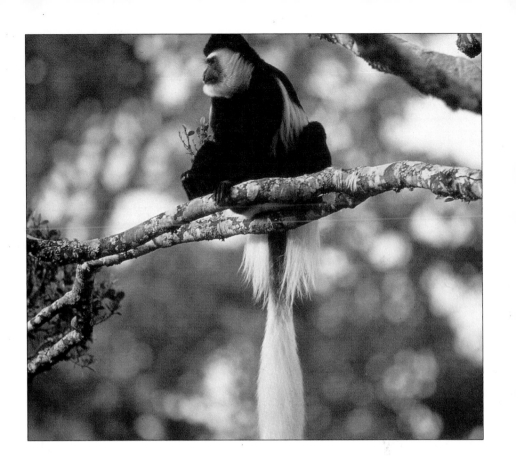

How can you tell an ape
from a monkey?  If it has
a tail, it's not an ape.

Apes never have tails.
And apes are bigger
than monkeys.

A full-grown male gorilla
is about as tall as a man.

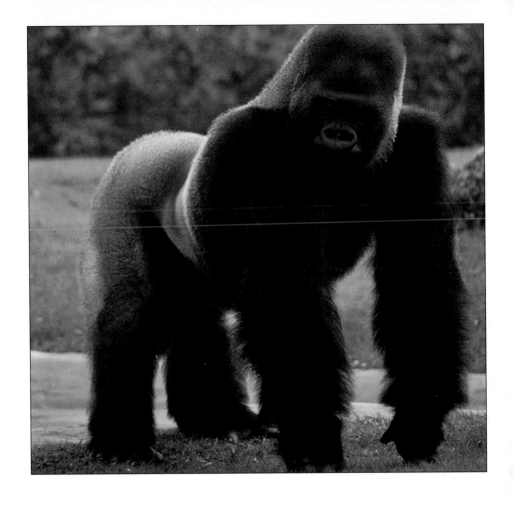

But a gorilla weighs two or three times more than a man.

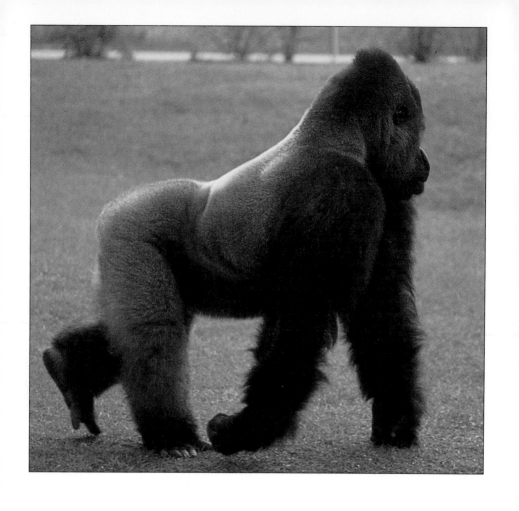

Though gorillas are able to
stand, they walk on all fours.

They keep their hands
bent when they walk,
so their knuckles touch
the ground.

Try walking that way.
It's hard for you...but
easy for a gorilla, because
a gorilla's arms are much
longer than its legs.

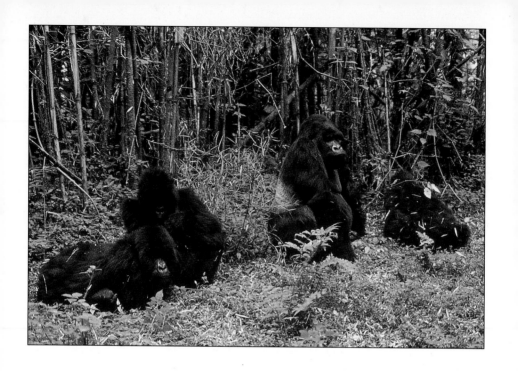

Gorillas in the wild live in
groups called troops. An
older male, with silver hair
on his back, is the leader
of each troop.

To make sure gorillas do not die out, some of their homelands in Africa are now protected.

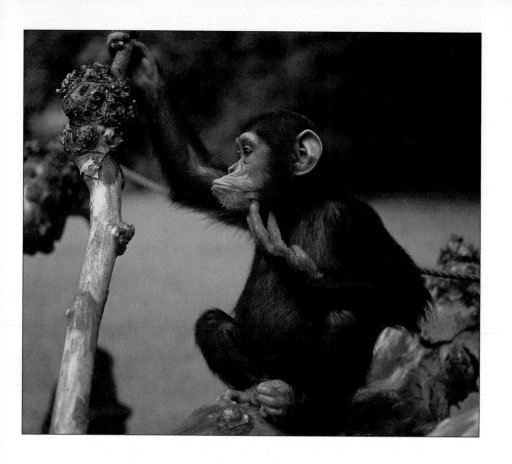

Besides gorillas, there
are three other kinds of
apes – chimpanzees,

orangutans, and gibbons.

17

Chimpanzees, like gorillas, come from Africa and live in troops.

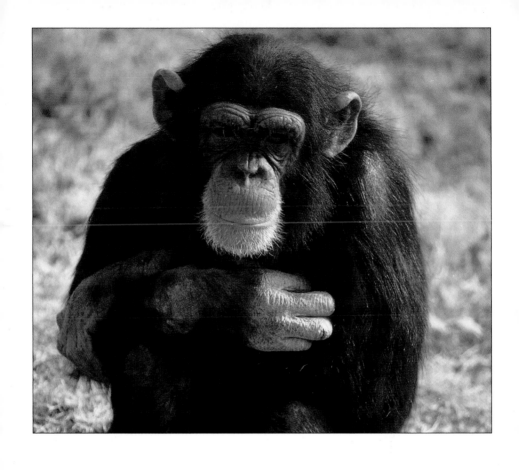

They are smaller than gorillas, but have bigger ears.

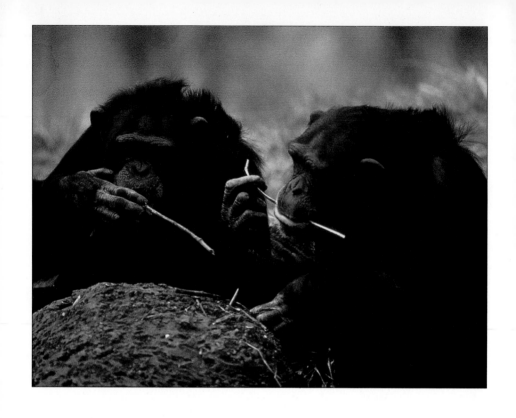

Chimpanzees, or chimps,
are the smartest of all
the apes. They use twigs
as tools to help them eat.

This chimp has even
been taught to "talk"
with people – by using
sign language.

Orangutans, too, are very smart and can be taught things. Their hair is reddish-brown.

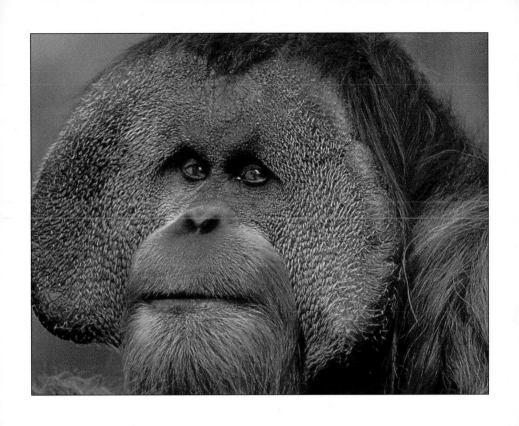

It's easy to tell the females
and males apart.  The males
have big pouches of skin
on their faces.

Orangutans live in
the forests of Borneo
and Sumatra.

Those are islands near
Southeast Asia.

Not far away, on the
Asian mainland, are the
forests where gibbons live.

Gibbons are the
smallest apes.

They spend most
of their time in trees.

Gibbons walk along the
branches on their two legs –
or swing from branch to
branch, using their long,
strong arms.

Chimps and orangutans
also swing through
the trees.

But you won't see adult
gorillas doing that.

They're so heavy that
they'd break the branches.

# Words You Know

Apes are found in Africa, Asia, Sumatra, and Borneo.

gorilla

chimpanzee (chimp)

orangutan

gibbons

primate

monkey

troop

31

# Index

## About the Author

Allan Fowler is a free-lance writer with a background in advertising. Born in New York, he lives in Chicago now and enjoys traveling.

## Photo Credits

Animals Animals – ©H.S. Terrace, 21

©Carl Purcell – 12

Tom Stack & Associates – ©Larry Tackett, 17 (left); ©Denise Tackett, 17 (right); ©Brian Parker, 23, 31 (top left)

SuperStock International, Inc. – 16; ©Alan Briere, Cover; ©Deborah Levinson, 7, 31 (center left); ©Roy King, 18, 19, 30 (bottom right); ©B. Amadeus Rubel, 22

Valan – ©Kennon Cooke, 5, 25, 26, 30 (bottom left), 31 (top right); ©John Cancalosi, 8, 29; ©James D. Markou, 9, 31 (center right); ©Robert C. Simpson, 11

Visuals Unlimited – ©Science VU, 3; ©Joe McDonald, 4; ©Walt Anderson, 15

The Wildlife Collection – ©Martin Harvey, 14, 31 (bottom); ©John Giustina, 20

Beth Herman Design Associates – map 30

COVER: Mountain Gorilla